W9-DAE-920

WITHDRAWN

# Maryland
## The Old Line State

Marcia Amidon Lusted

PowerKiDS press

New York

Published in 2010 by The Rosen Publishing Group, Inc.
29 East 21st Street, New York, NY 10010

First Edition

Editor: Nicole Pristash
Book Layout: Julio Gil
Book Design: Greg Tucker
Photo Researcher: Jessica Gerweck

Photo Credits: Cover © Fridmar Damm/zefa/Corbis; p. 5 © Heeb Christian/age fotostock; p. 7 © SuperStock; pp. 9, 22 (Harriet Tubman) MPI/Getty Images; p. 11 © SuperStock/age fotostock; p. 13 (main) Cameron Davidson/Getty Images; p. 13 (inset) © www.iStockphoto.com/Sandy Franz; pp. 15, 22 (bird) © www.iStockphoto.com/Bill Raboin; p. 17 Mark Wilson/Getty Images; pp. 19, 22 (tree, flag, flower) Shutterstock.com; p. 22 (Babe Ruth) Mark Rucker/Transcendental Graphics/Getty Images; p. 22 (Penn Badgley) Ray Tamarra/Getty Images.

Library of Congress Cataloging-in-Publication Data

Lusted, Marcia Amidon.
  Maryland : the Old Line State / Marcia Amidon Lusted. — 1st ed.
      p. cm. — (Our amazing states)
  Includes index.
  ISBN 978-1-4358-9350-4 (library binding) — ISBN 978-1-4358-9794-6 (pbk.) — ISBN 978-1-4358-9795-3 (6-pack)
  1. Maryland—Juvenile literature. I. Title.
  F181.3.L87 2010
  975.2—dc22

                                        2009030280

Manufactured in the United States of America

CPSIA Compliance Information: Batch #WW10PK: For Further Information contact Rosen Publishing, New York, New York at 1-800-237-9932

# Contents

# The Great State of Maryland

In which state can you eat crab cakes and see wild ponies on an island? In this state, you can hike the Appalachian Mountains and rest on a beach. Which state are we in? We are in Maryland!

Maryland is found on the Atlantic coast in between the northern and southern parts of the United States. Maryland has a straight northern border, but the bottom of the state has two armlike parts that surround Chesapeake Bay.

Even though Maryland is a small state, it has played a big part in U.S. history. Around 1790, Maryland **donated** the land that became Washington, D.C., America's capital!

4

Annapolis, Maryland, shown here, is the capital of Maryland. The city sits on Chesapeake Bay, which is a popular place for sailing.

# Maryland's Past

The first people to live in the area that is now Maryland were hunter-gatherer tribes who arrived more than 10,000 years ago. These people hunted buffalo and **mammoths** in the area. Later tribes fished for **oysters** in Chesapeake Bay.

In 1608, Captain John Smith became one of the first British explorers to enter the Chesapeake Bay area. In 1632, Maryland became a British colony. During the **American Revolution**, Maryland was known for its brave soldiers, known as the Maryland Line. It is said that General George Washington called the soldiers the Old Line, and this is how Maryland got its nickname, the Old Line State. Maryland then became the seventh state of the United States in 1788.

This painting shows a meeting between British settlers and Native Americans on St. Clement's Island, in the new Maryland Colony.

# War in Maryland

During the **Civil War**, soldiers from Maryland fought on both sides. Those who supported the South did not want to be a part of the Union, or country, anymore. They felt that each state should have its own rights. Those who supported the North wanted to keep the Union together. Some Northerners supported ending slavery. However, many Southerners owned slaves, and they did not want to lose them.

One of the bloodiest battles of the war took place at Antietam Creek, in central Maryland, on September 17, 1862. More than 23,000 soldiers were hurt or killed. The North won by keeping the South from coming into Northern territory. Maryland played a big part in U.S. history that day.

8

Here you can see the Northern army (left) taking over a bridge and charging at the Southern army (right) during the Battle of Antietam Creek.

# Water and Heat

Maryland is a small state. It is around 250 miles (402 km) long and about 100 miles (161 km) wide. The center of the state is a flat **plateau** that is good for farming. The nearby Potomac River winds along Maryland's southern border.

The eastern part of the state has the Chesapeake Bay, Maryland's largest body of water. This area is sometimes called the Tidewater **region** because the ocean tides in the bay sometimes change the shape of the land.

The weather in Maryland changes as you move from west to east. The western part of the state has cold winters and warm summers. The eastern part has cool winters and hot, humid summers.

The woman shown here is paddling a small boat called a kayak along the Potomac River. The river is a popular place for boating.

# A Very Crabby Bay

Maryland's Chesapeake Bay is the largest estuary in the United States. An estuary is a place where salt water from the ocean meets **freshwater** from rivers. Chesapeake Bay is about 200 miles (322 km) long.

Because it is an estuary, Chesapeake Bay has many different kinds of plants and animals. Jellyfish, oysters, and blue crabs live with freshwater creatures, such as striped bass, frogs, and salamanders. Bald eagles and seagulls live along its shorelines.

Chesapeake Bay has several important ports that are used for shipping. Its waters produce millions of pounds (kg) of seafood, and it is famous for its blue crabs. Many people also use the bay for boating, fishing, and swimming.

Here you can see the Chesapeake Bay at sunset. *Inset:* A blue crab walks along the sand.

# Forests, Ponies, and the Oriole

Even though Maryland has a large body of water and is near the ocean, forests cover much of the state. More than 150 different kinds of trees grow there, such as maple, oak, and pine. Flowers, such as black-eyed Susans and asters, are found in fields.

Maryland does not have many large animals. Smaller animals, such as birds, are plentiful. Maryland's state bird is the Baltimore oriole. Males have gold and black feathers. Females have brown and orange feathers. Maryland's most famous animals are the wild ponies of Assateague Island National Seashore. Assateague Island is a 37-mile- (60 km) long island off the coast of Maryland and Virginia. More than 300 wild ponies live there freely.

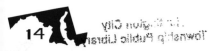

The Baltimore oriole mates, or makes babies, in Maryland during the summer. The bird then spends the rest of the year in Mexico and South America.

# Office Buildings and Fishing Boats

People who live in Maryland have many different types of jobs. Washington, D.C., is nearby, so many people in Maryland work for the U.S. government. Others in the state have jobs in which they create new **technologies** for NASA spaceflights or for the military.

Farming and fishing are popular jobs in Maryland as well. Farmers in Maryland grow corn and soybeans. The chicken you have for dinner may have even come from Maryland! Fishermen in Maryland make millions of dollars catching and selling blue crabs, clams, and oysters. Maryland crab cakes are famous all over the world. Half of all the blue crabs eaten in the United States come from Maryland.

These fishermen are catching crabs in Chesapeake Bay. The traps that crab fishermen use are called crab pots.

# Annapolis and Baltimore

Maryland's capital city is Annapolis. Annapolis is known for being the home of the United States Naval Academy. The Naval Academy is a school to which men and women go to become officers in the Navy.

Baltimore, which is north of Annapolis, is the largest city in Maryland. Baltimore's Inner Harbor has many restaurants and museums. You can visit the National Aquarium or watch the Baltimore Orioles baseball team play there. Near Baltimore is Fort McHenry. During the **War of 1812**, the British attacked the fort. This battle **inspired** Francis Scott Key to write a poem. The words of the poem would later become the words to "The Star-Spangled Banner," America's national anthem.

Baltimore has so many different areas that the city is often called the City of Neighborhoods. The area shown here is downtown.

# Come to Maryland!

Maryland has many fun and interesting things to do. You can visit a **replica** of the *Maryland Dove*, a famous ship that brought settlers to the state, in St. Marys City. You can go to a restaurant and eat crab cakes, one of Maryland's most famous dishes. Crab cakes are made of crabmeat and bread crumbs, among other things. Visitors to the National Aquarium, in Baltimore, can see sharks, eels, and dolphins. You can also visit the National Museum of **Dentistry**, in Baltimore, and see George Washington's false teeth!

Maryland has a lot to offer. Whether you want to explore the history of the United States, enjoy nature, or eat some tasty seafood, Maryland is a great place to be!

# Glossary

**American Revolution** (uh-MER-uh-ken reh-vuh-LOO-shun)  Battles that soldiers from the colonies fought against Britain for freedom, from 1775 to 1783.

**Civil War** (SIH-vul WOR)  The war fought between the Northern and the Southern states of America, from 1861 to 1865.

**dentistry** (DEN-tuh-stree)  The practice of taking care of people's teeth and mouths.

**donated** (DOH-nayt-ed)  Gave something away.

**freshwater** (FRESH-wah-ter)  Water without salt.

**inspired** (in-SPY-urd)  Moved someone to do something.

**mammoths** (MA-muths)  Ancient elephants with long, curving tusks and brown hair.

**oysters** (OYS-terz)  Flat shellfish that have shells made up of two parts that come together at one end.

**plateau** (pla-TOH)  A broad, flat, high piece of land.

**region** (REE-jun)  A different part of Earth.

**replica** (REH-plih-kuh)  An exact copy of an object used in the past.

**technologies** (tek-NAH-luh-jeez)  The ways that people do things using tools and the tools that they use.

**War of 1812** (WOR UV AY-teen TWELV)  A war between the United States and Britain, fought from 1812 to 1815.

# Maryland State Symbols

State Tree
White Oak

State Dog
Chesapeake Bay
Retriever

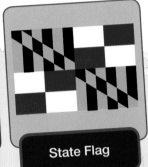
State Flag

State Bird
Baltimore Oriole

State Flower
Black-Eyed Susan

State Seal

## Famous People from Maryland

**Harriet Tubman**
(Around 1820–1913)
Born in Dorchester County, MD
Abolitionist

**Babe Ruth**
(1895–1948)
Born in Baltimore, MD
Baseball Player

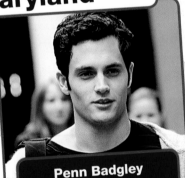
**Penn Badgley**
(1986– )
Born in Baltimore, MD
Actor

# Maryland State Map

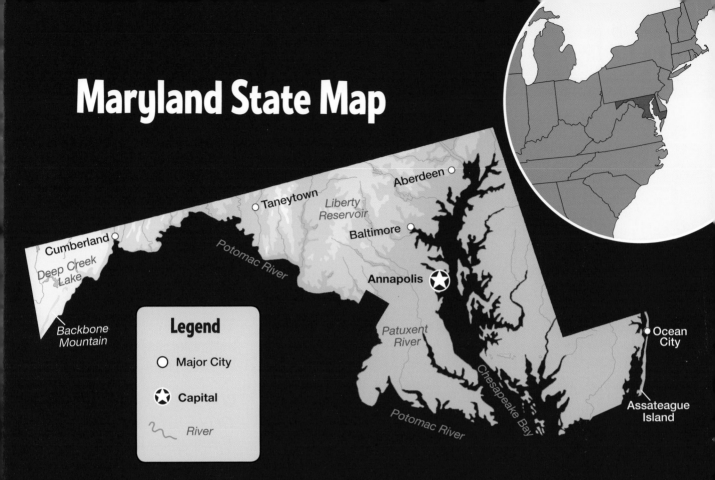

Cumberland

Deep Creek
Lake

Backbone
Mountain

Taneytown

Liberty
Reservoir

Potomac River

Aberdeen

Baltimore

Annapolis

Patuxent
River

Potomac River

Chesapeake Bay

Ocean
City

Assateague
Island

### Legend

○ Major City

⭐ Capital

〜 River

# Maryland State Facts

**Population:** About 5,296,516

**Area:** 10,460 square miles (27,091 sq km)

**Motto:** "Fatti maschii parole femine" ("Manly deeds, womanly words")

**Song:** "Maryland, My Maryland," words by James Ryder Randall

# Index

**A**
Appalachian Mountains, 4

**B**
battle(s), 8, 18
beach, 4
border, 4, 10

**C**
capital, 4
Chesapeake Bay, 4, 6, 10, 12
Civil War, 8
coast, 4, 14
crab cakes, 4, 16, 20

**H**
history, 4, 8, 20

**I**
island, 4, 14

**L**
land, 4, 10

**M**
mammoths, 6

**N**
National Aquarium, 18, 20
National Museum of Dentistry, 20

**O**
oysters, 6, 12, 16

**P**
people, 6, 12, 16
plateau, 10

**R**
replica, 20

**S**
soldiers, 6, 8

**T**
technologies, 16
Tidewater region, 10

**W**
War of 1812, 18
Washington, D.C., 4, 16

# Web Sites

Due to the changing nature of Internet links, PowerKids Press has developed an online list of Web sites related to the subject of this book. This site is updated regularly. Please use this link to access the list:

www.powerkidslinks.com/amst/md/